Renewing Vows

An Essential Guide to Celebrating the Renewal of Wedding Vows

by Patricia Bosley

Table of Contents

Introduction

Are you thinking of a way to show your partner that you want your relationship to remain solid and committed? If you've been married a while, one of the best (and most fun) ways to do this is by planning to renew your vows. A wedding vow renewal can be anything you want it to be; and in some ways it's even more about you and your partner than your wedding day was.

It's never too soon or too late to plan your vow renewal ceremony. Whether you've been together two years or fifty, your relationship has flourished during good times together and survived when circumstances were hard. Your vow renewal is a milestone celebration of all that you have done together and all that you will do in the future.

You may be thinking that your reason for wanting the ceremony isn't enough. But there are plenty of reasons people renew vows: If you didn't have the wedding you wanted the first time around, now you'll have an opportunity to do exactly as you please. If you've made some monumental decision together, and find yourself wanting to celebrate, it's the perfect occasion. Maybe your relationship is starting anew, or you're just excited that your love still feels fresh. All of these are excellent reasons to renew your vows.

Chapter 1: Where to Start the Planning

Figuring out the mood of your event is the easiest way to get things started. Once you know what look and feel you want for your ceremony, you'll be better able to make the big decisions.

One of the first things to consider is your personal reason for the renewal. If you're doing this to start fresh with your marriage, you may want the mood be more serious or formal. If you're celebrating, or planning to have the wedding you always wanted, you may have a bit more of a party atmosphere.

If you don't know exactly what you want, consider some creative ways to brainstorm. For example, if you are a visual learner, try organizing your thoughts using a mood board. A mood board is a fashion technique, but I find that it is a wonderful tool, useful for all sorts of projects. Think of it as a professional form of scrapbooking. Traditionally, mood boards were done using large pieces of foam or cardboard, onto which images corresponding to the idea were glued. It's a tool that can help you narrow down ideas visually, by discovering the similarities and differences between things you're picking. Make a separate one for each factor. These could include color palette, food choices, decorations, locations… anything you need inspiration for when making your celebration decisions.

You and your partner should do this together to get an idea of what you each want. It can help you both iron out expectations beforehand so there are no surprises later. If you're not agreeing on any specific factor of the ceremony, it'll be much easier to discuss and compromise while things are in the planning stages, and not after money has been spent. It's also just a fun bonding experience. Head over to your local craft store and grab some foam core, mat board, or a presentation display board and have fun! Or, if the two of you are more technologically inclined, feel free to use sites like Tumblr or Pinterest. Either way, you'll be surprised how much visual representation can help you figure out what you want. If you don't feel like making your own mood board, go onto Tumblr and Pinterest and use keywords to see what other people have come up with.

Ask friends who have had a vow renewal for their input. Finally, you can search your favorite bridal magazines online to see if they have any articles published on vow renewals. Even searching wedding trends can be helpful, because after all, vow renewals can be very similar to traditional weddings.

Chapter 2: Establishing Your Budget

What does your budget look like? Even if you plan on going all out, it's good to be realistic. Don't plan to have an event that's so over the top, you're stressing for money during and after. Alternately, if you're worried you won't have enough money to host the party you want, don't fret. DIY is always in style, and even if you don't consider yourself to be very creative, you can enlist some creative friends to help. No matter your budget, this event should be a positive, fun experience, not an added stressor.

Your Baseline Budget

At the early stages of planning, don't worry about doing perfectly accurate math; think of your overall budget, and then divide that number up roughly according to what you feel is important. Some things to consider while planning are: refreshments for the guests, cake, formal attire (if desired), decorations, entertainment, and location. If you're a visual person, you could easily make a pie chart to give you an idea of how much money is to be spent where. You could also use an Excel spreadsheet, or a simple list. However you do this, put the beginnings of your budget in a safe place so that you can reference it later. This is very important to do early on, since caterers, venues, and guests all need to be notified months in advance to be adequately prepared.

Having figured out your baseline budget, determine what to tackle first. Every couple is different, but for most, the major concerns are location and food. I would suggest deciding on these two first before you consider your guest list. This way, you know how many guests you can feasibly invite. Knowing that you can only fit 75 people into a venue as opposed to 150 makes it easier to determine who you really want to invite. If you start with creating your guest list first, you may find that you cannot afford to feed or entertain that many people, and then have to narrow it down.

If you are planning to have a destination vow renewal, it's even more important to figure out how many people you can invite. You'll need to take into consideration that some of the people who may be the closest to you might need help paying for travel, and if you really want them to be there, you should be prepared to take on some of that expense.

Food and Refreshments

Unless you already know a specific caterer or service you would like to use, shop around a bit to find the perfect fit for your tastes and budget. Food and beverages will often require more money than anything else on your expense list. Keep in mind that while catering companies will have a number of set menus, many offer mix and match options. Caterers also need to know what is expected of them ahead of time. Even though some places are beginning to offer ready-made menus that can be picked up on short notice, don't depend on that. Typically, there is a waitlist, especially if it's a popular company. Waitlist times vary, but can be months long, particularly during popular wedding months.

Busy months vary, depending on where you're located, but are typically during summer and early fall months, or December. If you intend to have your vow renewal around one of these times, you really have to be on top of your planning. Do your research ahead of time and if there are a few places you're interested in, see if you can schedule with the company to do a tasting, and confirm the waitlist or preparation time with them. The same tactic is also applicable to cakes. It's important to remember that if you are hiring a caterer or renting a venue, it is likely they will ask you to put down an advance deposit to hold your reservation.

Another popular option that gets guests involved, and is more economical, is to hold a dinner or potluck. This can work out especially well for smaller, more intimate parties. Asking friends who are talented in cooking and baking for recipes or to help in preparing a menu is more cost effective than going with a caterer. If you choose to go the potluck route, settle on a theme for the dinner and then ask your guests to provide a specified dish, beverage, or other necessary item.

The Venue

The same general idea goes for locations. It's important to know how many people can safely be accommodated in the venue, how long the venue can be reserved for, and whether it will work for your needs. If you have your venue reserved for a set block of time, consider that that time includes set up and take down. If these tasks are work intensive, and the venue doesn't provide workers to help you, factor that into your budget. Also ask whether things such as tables, tablecloths and chairs are provided. If not, consider the cost. Keep in mind, while searching for your venue, that an all-inclusive package deal with a higher price tag may or may not be more cost effective than having to talk to different suppliers for everything you need in the venue. Take note of what services or extras come with the venue and compare costs. It won't hurt to ask for additional inclusions too. (Maybe you can get to use the sound system or DJ booth free?)

An option for those with a smaller budget is to hold the event at your house. If your backyard is nice, renting awnings and having a wedding arch built would be less expensive than the rental costs of a space. Your vow renewal could even be held in your house, if you have a spacious living room or screened in porch.

After location and food are taken care of, remember to set a budget for smaller expenses: attire, entertainment, decorations, or maybe new rings for yourself and your partner. All of these may not apply, but it's important to think about it so you don't run into complications later on.

Chapter 3: How to Give Your Renewal Ceremony a Unique Feel

You'll want to make sure to differentiate your vow renewal from your wedding. Remember that this is a confirmation of an existing relationship, a reaffirmation. As such, it should be treated differently. There are of course hundreds of different ways to go about this. One suggestion is to do the opposite of what you did for your wedding. So, if you couldn't afford a big, formal event the first time around, go for it. Pick bridesmaids and groomsmen and wedding colors. Have a giant cake and a first dance.

Alternatively, if you've been married a decade or two, perhaps your vow renewal should be an intimate affair. In this case I would suggest only inviting those close to you; parents, people who acted as witnesses or bridesmaids/groomsmen at your wedding, close friends that you may have made since you married. There is no need this time to invite that distant cousin or your boss; if they haven't been important to one or both of you during your time together. If you want to trim down your guests to only those who really need to be there, ask yourself if that someone has had an impact in your married life. The people who have supported you, who would be happy to know you are renewing your commitment as a couple, are the folk you want to be with on this day.

Attire is also up for question here. A wedding dress certainly isn't required, unless you want one. If you do, consider wearing a non-white dress. Recently, pale colored dresses in off-white, beige, grey, purple, pink, green, and yellow have been incredibly popular. Often, women who are going into a marriage that isn't their first choose to wear them. It's especially appropriate if you're older.

If the idea of the cost and hassle of fittings have you shaking your head, formal wear with an accent in your wedding colors would be a nice touch.

Next, consider how formal your guests should be. Unless you and your partner have decided to go all the way to jeans-and-t-shirt casual, asking them to wear their Sunday best is acceptable. As for former bridesmaids/groomsmen, their dress is really dependent on yours, and on the role they'll be expected to play in the ceremony. If you're only going to wear a nice dress or suit, asking them to all have matching dresses and suits again is a bit much. However, requesting them to add a pop of your wedding colors is a cute touch, especially if they will be standing in front of the altar again.

A vow renewal is also a great occasion to get new rings or have the old ones cleaned up. Perhaps purchase better quality rings, or update your style if the old one no longer fits.

If you like the idea of exchanging rings again, but don't feel that you need or want to, consider exchanging some other gift. Traditionally, gifts can range from paper for the first anniversary to aluminum to pearls and diamonds. While these may sound like odd things (I certainly don't suggest handing your partner a hunk of wood as a gift), they can be used as the source of inspiration when picking out your gifts for each other. See how closely your vow renewal date corresponds to an anniversary and use that to guide you. If you get bronze, for example, consider purchasing things like metal jewelry, watches, or a piece of sculpture.

Children can also play an important part in the ceremony, if you have them. They are important to your marriage and should be acknowledged. Younger children could play the role of flower girls or boys, or as ring bearers or gift bearers. Older (or adult) children could stand up at the altar with you and your partner, either with or in place of your original wedding party.

Every good wedding demands a good speech, so you might consider allowing your children to prepare something as a prelude to your vows. This could be anything from a traditional speech or toast, to a picture slideshow of moments that were important to the family as a whole, to a recorded video or even a Skype chat if the person is physically unable to attend.

There are certain wedding traditions that are not necessarily applicable to a vow renewal ceremony. In addition to wearing a color other than white, there are a few other traditions that should be mentioned as well. Bachelor's/Bachelorette parties are just that: for people who haven't been married before. Hosting another such party would seem quite inappropriate and out of place when the focus should be on commitment.

Gifts, too, may be out of place. Traditionally, gifts are given to a young couple just starting out. Odds are, you and your partner don't need to furnish your home at this point. Exceptions to this rule exist, however. If you are announcing a new baby, it might be appropriate to request baby shower gifts, for example.

Chapter 4: Creating Personal Renewal Vows

After logistics and budgets, your actual vows are the most important part of the ceremony to consider. It is certainly the most important emotional aspect. Since the very focus is in the name of the thing, using only the traditional wedding vows isn't recommended, although you can if you choose to. If you are particularly religious or traditional, having traditional vows read by a member of your chosen clergy would be understandable. If you would like to have a member of clergy present, be sure you talk to them about your preferred dates and times as early as possible to confirm they are available. Whether religious or secular, though, you should consider incorporating vows that you have written yourself.

If you already did this when you got married, think of this as your updated vows. If this is your first time writing vows, consider that this is, in some ways, a much more special occasion than your wedding day because it celebrates the flourishing of your relationship.

Most people, upon being asked to write something, will protest that they can't write or speak in front of people. These are understandable and common fears, but expressing your deepest emotions to your spouse is a far cry from speech class in college. Know that you can either read your vows straight after you write them, or that you can use it as a guide to prepare the general idea of what you want to say. I would strongly suggest the latter, simply because you don't want this very meaningful moment to sound rehearsed or fake. It's better to allow your emotions to take you where they will when the time comes for you to speak.

If you're stuck for vow ideas, reflect on things you and your spouse have gone through together: an anecdote that's important to you, the reasons for your renewal, things you are grateful for, and vows you want to work on or attach special importance to.

At weddings, many couples will tell a story about how they met. If you've recently been married, this may still be relevant, but if you have been through a lot since then, perhaps talk about something you went through together that made you experience falling in love with your partner again. Talk about how your relationship has changed or deepened with time.

The reason for your vow renewal is also important. Often, your friends and guests may be curious as to why you are having this event now or at all. Of course, if you'd like to keep the reason between yourself and your partner, you can do so, but people love a reason to celebrate. This time could be used to make a big announcement, such as a move, a new job, or a new baby. If your marriage has seen some tough moments, now may be the time to publicly acknowledge your intention of moving past them. If this is the case, be sure to keep it positive.

Tell your partner all of the reasons you love for having him or her in your life. Don't just stick to basic qualities such as loyalty or honesty, although those are important to mention especially if they are particularly relevant. Mention the little things about them, habits or gestures they have that you weren't aware of when you first married. Talk about the little things they do for you each day that have made your relationship special. Don't focus on disagreements, fights, or how tough things may have been in the past.

Finally, if there are specific issues you each want to work on, reiterate that in your vows. You may say, "I'll work on being more patient," or "I'll be more attentive," or "Date night will become a regular event."

No matter what is said, address what's closest to your heart. Embrace your vow renewal as fully as you can.

Chapter 5: Planning the Little Details

After planning the major parts of your event, it's time to start inviting people. If your budget and location hasn't already forced you to figure out about 80 percent of your guest list, you should draw that up now. Because renewal ceremonies are more intimate, milestone events, consider that only the people who first occur to you and your partner should be invited. The only exceptions to this rule might be important family members who, while you may not have the best relationship, if not invited, will make you look rude. If this is the case, think of this as an occasion to perhaps also heal that rift.

Invitations

You might be wondering how best to go about making your invitations. These days, nearly everyone has a Facebook account, so making sure to send around an event invite is crucial. For smaller parties, a private group can be created for your guests. This way, other friends and acquaintances who may not have been invited won't be upset.

While Facebook provides convenience and an assurance that most guests will receive their invitation, it's still nice (and classy) for people to get an invitation in the mail. There are lots of options at many different price points online. Invitations can be ordered from familiar names such as David's Bridal and Vistaprint. Some companies specialize in wedding invitations that are customizable to a point and come in different price point categories.

For a really unique invitation, working with an artist to come up with a design helps stimulate your local economy by helping the artist get their work out to people who may not otherwise see it. Don't know of any local artists? Look up galleries around your area and see if you can find an artist whose work you adore. Barring that, use a site such as DeviantArt or Etsy, which will put you in touch with local and international artists. Keep in mind that if you choose a completely customizable option like this, you're typically paying for a much higher standard of work, which, of course, makes the work more expensive. The upside to paying a higher price is that you'll have an invitation that becomes a keepsake. You can also find any style or qualification you may be looking for, including things like: recycled or bio-friendly materials, cruelty free inks, or products that fund causes you support.

Once you've chosen where to purchase your invitations, consider how you want them to look. Go back to your mood board and select at most, three compatible colors. Keep it simple, and to your style. You don't want to overwhelm the viewer. As mentioned before, if you already have wedding colors, make use of them. Make sure that you pick a font that is both elegant and legible. You may want the front script or your names in a cursive style, but be sure that the important information is written in a simple, clear font. Double-check the date, time, venue, and other important specifications before sending them to print. Luckily, most places will email you a proof 24 hours after your order is placed, so you'll be able to catch any mistakes there.

Decorations

Where decorations are concerned, there are lots and lots of options available today. If you have the budget to hire a wedding planner or decorator, they can take on that responsibility for you. Of course, you should give them access to your mood boards, color palette, budget, and any other planning materials that will make their job easier.

For most people, DIY decorations are much more economically feasible. Since your theme will already be solidly in place at this point, choosing decorations should be fairly simple. Flowers are, of course, the first staple of wedding decoration that comes to mind. The immediate thought is to go to a florist and have them arrange bouquets and/or table settings. It's elegant and timeless to do so, but may also push you over budget, particularly if the flowers you want aren't in season or aren't readily available where you live. Plus, you're paying someone to do the arrangements.

Several other options exist. Elegant potted plants could be purchased, and then given as gifts to your guests or donated to a local organization that you support after your celebration is finished. My favorite style of potted plants is the hanging pots, which would be really cute for an outdoor spring or summer event. Alternative to live plants, silk or dried flowers can be used again, and may save you money overall. Dried flowers are definitely gorgeous for fall or winter weddings and renewals. Finally, if you're artsy or particularly environmentally conscious, you may want to get together with some friends and create "floral arrangements" made from paper, scraps of fabric, and other recyclable materials. This option is great if you have small children and want to get them involved in the planning.

Other decorative choices will depend on the mood and style of your vow renewal. For an outdoor setting, tea lights, lanterns, and candles create a festive atmosphere. It is important to find out in advance what kinds of things or materials are permissible as décor when planning to decorate an indoor rented venue. Some places, especially if they are historical buildings, have restrictions against streamers or banners. Also, it's just rude to get glitter all over the place, because it can never all be swept up.

Music and Entertainment

The best part of a wedding is the after party, and I feel the same should go for a vow renewal. Never book your entertainment last minute, especially during wedding seasons, or you may find yourselves with a bad Beatles cover band. Consider whether a live band or a DJ would be more appropriate for the mood of your ceremony.

When searching for musicians, be sure to ask them for a sample of their music. It's also a good idea to ask if you can come and watch them perform before you make a final decision, to make sure they are exactly what you want live. If you like their sound, approach them with a repertoire of the kinds of music you would like played and have them confirm. Just as with everything else, it's very likely that you will need to put down a deposit to hold your date. In addition, you should ask them whether they will be bringing the equipment they need, or if a rental is required. If it is, it may come as a part of the performance price or an added fee. The venue you have rented may also have the required equipment if the band doesn't. Make sure you ask them how much setup and takedown time is required and factor that into your decision. To finalize everything, make sure there is a written contract of agreement.

Photography

One last detail you'll want to be sure not to forget is a photographer to capture special moments during the event. With the advent of social media, it seems everyone thinks they are a photographer, but this is a moment you'll want professionally done. When looking for a photographer, try to find someone who either specializes in wedding and event photography, or has a style you're in love with. Keep in mind that their asking price, unless otherwise stated on their website or to you, is probably by the hour. This means that you'll have to pay an additional fee for post processing and for prints, if you want them. Package prices can be helpful, and don't be afraid to ask your photographer for more information.

Conclusion

So, you've done it. What started as a thought and a mood board has come to fruition. You've decided your date, booked your caterer and venue, found a DJ, photographer, and florist, and everything is beautiful.

Once you've got your event planned and executed, focus on your vows and let everything else go. Enjoy the day and let it center on the commitment you and your partner have to each other. When that love shines through, it's sure to be a successful celebration.

With these easy steps, you should be able to successfully plan your event, with a little help from those you love, of course. Should little snags prop up on the day itself, as they tend to, remember that what's important is you are able to laugh it off with a loving, committed partner who will be by your side for better or for worse.

Finally, I'd like to thank you for purchasing this book! If you enjoyed it or found it helpful, I'd greatly appreciate it if you'd take a moment to leave a review on Amazon. Thank you!

Made in United States
Orlando, FL
01 June 2024

47430931R00024